Encounters with God

The Epistle of Paul the Apostle to the COLOSSIANS and PHILEMON

Encounters with God Study Guide Series

The Gospel of Matthew

The Gospel of Mark

The Gospel of Luke

The Gospel of John

The Acts of the Apostles

The Book of Romans

The First Epistle of Paul the Apostle to the Corinthians

The Second Epistle of Paul the Apostle to the Corinthians

The Epistle of Paul the Apostle to the Galatians

The Epistle of Paul the Apostle to the Ephesians

The Epistle of Paul the Apostle to the Philippians

The Epistle of Paul the Apostle to the Colossians and Philemon

Encounters with God

The Epistle of Paul the Apostle to the COLOSSIANS and PHILEMON

Published by Thomas Nelson, Inc., P.O. Box 141000, Nashville, Tennessee 37214.

Scripture quotations are taken from The New King James Version® (NKJV), copyright 1979, 1980, 1982, 1992 Thomas Nelson, Inc., Publishers.

Library of Congress Cataloging-in-Publication Data
ISBN 1-4185-26495

Printed in the United States of America

08 09 10 RRD 9 8 7 6 5 4 3 2 1

All Scripture references are from the New King James Version of the Bible.

Contents

An Introduction to the Epistles of Colossians and Philemon 7

An Overview of Our Study of the Epistles of Colossians and Philemon 11

The Lessons:

    LESSON #1: Effective Prayer for Others 15

    LESSON #2: The Supremacy of Christ Jesus 25

    LESSON #3: The Limitations of Legalism 35

    LESSON #4: Putting Off the Old Nature 47

    LESSON #5: Putting On a New Nature 57

    LESSON #6: The Christian Home 67

    LESSON #7: How to Treat Those Who Serve You or Rule over You 75

Notes to Leaders of Small Groups 87

AN INTRODUCTION TO THE EPISTLES OF COLOSSIANS AND PHILEMON

This study guide covers two of the epistles from the apostle Paul—one to the church at Colosse and another to an individual named Philemon. Both are very short letters written from Paul while he was imprisoned in Rome, approximately 60–64 AD.

Colosse was strategically situated in the Lycus Valley in the region of Phrygia, about a hundred miles east of Ephesus. This city, historically, had played a prominent role in the Persian wars of the fifth century before Christ. It was located on a trade route and had once been a major commercial center. By the time of Paul, the city was in decline and had lost much of its earlier influence. It was overshadowed in both size and importance by two sister cities, Laodicea and Hierapolis. During Paul's three years of ministry and teaching in Ephesus, one of his converts, Epaphras, took the gospel to Colosse. Epaphras became an influential church leader there and also apparently evangelized Laodicea and Hierapolis as well. Although Paul apparently never visited Colosse, his colleague Timothy seems to have helped evangelize the city.

The church at Colosse was predominantly Gentile. The city had a lingering fervent paganism and Paul wrote, in part, to warn strongly against the influence of ungodly beliefs and practices. Specifically, a heresy seems to have infiltrated the church. False teachers were requiring a strict obligation to certain foods and drinks, a denial of the humanity of Christ, a "super-knowledge" of Christ that boasted of added wisdom and insight beyond the teachings of the apostles, and a digression from the supremacy of Christ and His sufficiency for all. Paul's letter urges the Colossians to preserve true doctrine.

The letter to the Colossians bears many similarities to the letter to the Ephesians. In fact, Colossians and Ephesians have 75 verses in common.

Both letters focus strongly on Christ and His relationship to the church. The letter to the Ephesians places greater focus on the glory of the *church* in its relationship to Christ, while the letter to the Colossians places greater emphasis on the glory of *Christ* and extends Christ's authority beyond the church to all creation. The two letters likely were written within the same year, along with the letter to Philemon. Most Bible teachers recommend that Colossians and Ephesians be studied together.

Paul called the Colossian church to become "complete" in Christ, and to apply Christ's work to every aspect of the Christian life: salvation, creation, reconciliation, service, holy living, and relationships at home and at work. In the minds of many Bible scholars, Colossians reflects the most complete understanding of Christ's nature and His relationship to believers personally and to the church corporately.

Paul's letter to Philemon—only one chapter with twenty-five verses— stands alone as a personal letter. It was not written to address a theological issue, or to correct sin or heresy. Rather, it was a plea for the life of a new brother in Christ. Onesimus, a runaway slave who appears to have stolen from his master, had been won by Paul to Christ. The acceptable punishment for such offenses was death. Paul, however, exhorted Philemon to see Onesimus as a spiritual brother, not as an unworthy slave. His letter of compassionate intervention is exemplary for all believers. It demonstrates, in a most practical way, the kind of Christian character that stood in marked contrast to Roman society. It is a statement that points toward inward trans- formation and personal sacrifice, and above all, forgiveness.

About the Author, the Apostle Paul. The author of both Colossians and Philemon was the apostle Paul, who was writing to a group of people whom he had never met, and to an individual that he knew well enough to call "beloved friend and fellow laborer." The two letters reflect a man who formed deep personal associations and, at the same time, had extensive influence over others who knew of his teachings and ministry but did not know him personally.

Paul's name was originally Saul (Acts 13:9), the royal name of Israel's first king. Upon his conversion, he adopted the name Paul, which literally meant "little" and reflected his self-evaluation as being "the least of the apostles" (1 Corinthians 15:98). Certainly in the history of Christianity, the "little" apostle became the foremost apostle to the Gentile world.

Paul was a Roman citizen, his hometown being Tarsus, the chief city of Cilicia. He was fluent in Greek, studied philosophy and theology under Gamaliel, and was also a Hebrew, the son of a Pharisee from the tribe of Benjamin. Paul, too, became a Pharisee, a very strict follower of Jewish religious laws. By trade, he was a tentmaker. This unique blend of cultural, religious, and experiential factors gave Paul unusual entrée into both Gentile and Jewish circles.

Initially, Paul was a major force in denouncing Christianity in Jerusalem, and had been a willing witness to Stephen's martyrdom. While on a mission to seek out and destroy Christians who had traveled to Syria, Paul had a dramatic encounter with the risen Christ. In the aftermath, he became as zealous a believer in Christ Jesus and advocate for the gospel as he once had been a determined foe of the early church. He took several fruitful and demanding missionary journeys, spending as long as two years in some areas to teach those who had heeded the gospel message and accepted Jesus as their Savior. Over the decades of his ministry, he became the most influential church planter and theologian in the early church. His letters addressed both the triumphs and difficulties encountered by the first-century Christians, many of whom faced intense persecution for their faith.

The issues that Paul addressed in his letters to the first-century church are no less important to today's believers. Paul laid a practical foundation for *how* to live the Christian life, even in the face of struggles, temptations, and heresies. His personal example of seeking to know and obey Christ Jesus, no matter what the cost, remains an example to all who call themselves Christians. "I in Christ and Christ in me" was Paul's unwavering theme song.

AN OVERVIEW OF OUR STUDY OF THE EPISTLES OF COLOSSIANS AND PHILEMON

This study guide presents seven lessons drawn from and based largely upon the epistles of Colossians and Philemon. The study guide elaborates upon, and is based upon, the commentary included in the Blackaby Study Bible:

Lesson #1: Effective Prayer for Others

Lesson #2: The Supremacy of Christ Jesus

Lesson #3: The Limitations of Legalism

Lesson #4: Putting Off the Old Nature

Lesson #5: Putting On a New Nature

Lesson #6: The Christian Home

Lesson #7: How to Treat Those Who Serve You or Rule Over You

Personal or Group Use. These lessons are offered for personal study and reflection or for small-group Bible study. The questions may be answered by an individual reader or used as a foundation for group discussion. A segment titled "Notes to Leaders of Small Groups" is included at the back of this book to help those who might lead a group study of the material.

Before you embark on this study, we encourage you to read in full "How to Study the Bible" in the *Blackaby Study Bible* on pages viii-ix. Our contention is always that the Bible is unique among all literature. It is God's definitive word for humanity. The Bible is:

- *inspired*—God breathed

- *authoritative*—absolutely the final word on any spiritual matter

- *the plumb line of truth*—the standard against which all human activity and reasoning must be evaluated

The Bible is fascinating in that it has remarkable diversity, but also remarkable unity. The books were penned by a diverse assortment of authors representing a variety of languages and cultures. The Bible as a whole has a number of literary forms. But, the Bible's message from cover to cover is clear, consistent, and unified.

More than mere words on a page, the Bible is an encounter with God Himself. No book is more critical to your life. The essence of the Bible is the Lord Himself.

God speaks by the Holy Spirit through the Bible. He also communicates during your time of prayer, in your life circumstances, and through the church. Read your Bible in an attitude of prayer and allow the Holy Spirit to make you aware of God's activity in and through your personal life. Write down what you learn, meditate on it, and adjust your thoughts, attitudes, and behavior accordingly. Look for ways every day in which the truth of God's Word can be applied to your circumstances and relationships. God is not random, but orderly and intentional in the way He speaks to you.

Be encouraged—the Bible is *not* too difficult for the average person to understand if that person asks the Holy Spirit for help. (Furthermore, not even the most brilliant person can fully understand the Bible apart from the Holy Spirit's help!) God desires for you to know Him and His Word. Everyone who reads the Bible can learn from it. The person who will receive maximum benefit from reading and studying the Bible, however, is the person who:

- *is born again* (John 3:3, 5). Those who are born again and have received the gift of God's Spirit have a distinct advantage in understanding the deeper truths of His Word.

- *has a heart that desires to learn God's truth.* Your attitude greatly influences the outcome of Bible study. Resist the temptation to focus on what others have said about the Bible. Allow the Holy Spirit to guide you as you study God's Word for yourself.

- *has a heart that seeks to obey God.* The Holy Spirit teaches most those who have a desire to apply what they learn. Begin your Bible study with prayer, asking the Holy Spirit to guide your thoughts and to impress on you what is on God's heart. Then, make plans to adjust your life immediately to obey the Lord fully.

As you read and study the Bible, your purpose is not to *create* meaning, but to *discover* the meaning of the text with the Holy Spirit's guidance. Ask yourself, "What did the author have in mind? How was this applied by those who first heard these words?" Especially in your study of the Gospel accounts, pay attention to the words of Jesus that begin "Most assuredly" or "He opened His mouth and taught them, saying." These are core principles and teachings that powerfully impact every person's life.

At times you may find it helpful to consult other passages of the Bible (made available in the center columns in the *Blackaby Study Bible*), or the commentary in the margins of the *Blackaby Study Bible.*

Keep in mind always that Bible study is not primarily an exercise for acquiring information, but it is an opportunity for transformation. Bible study is your opportunity to encounter God and to be changed in His presence. When God speaks to your heart, nothing remains the same. Jesus said, "He who has ears to hear, let him hear" (Matthew 13:9). Choose to have ears that desire to hear!

The B-A-S-I-Cs of Each Study in This Guide. Each lesson in this study guide has five segments, using the word BASIC as an acronym. The word BASIC does not allude to elementary or simple, but rather, to *foundational.* These studies extend the concepts that are part of the *Blackaby Study Bible* commentary and are focused on key aspects of what it means to be a Christ-follower in today's world. The BASIC acronym stands for:

B = Bible Focus. This segment presents the central passage for the lesson and a general explanation that covers the central theme or concern.

A = Application for Today. This segment has a story or illustration related to modern-day times, with questions that link the Bible text to today's issues, problems, and concerns.

S = Supplementary Scriptures to Consider. In this segment, other Bible verses related to the general theme of the lesson are explored.

I = Introspection and Implications. In this segment, questions are asked that lead to deeper reflection about one's personal faith journey and life experiences.

C = Communicating the Good News. This segment presents challenging questions aimed at ways in which the truth of the lesson might be lived out and shared with others (either to win the lost or build up the church).

Lesson #1
EFFECTIVE PRAYER FOR OTHERS

Prayer: petitioning God

B
Bible Focus

> *[We] do not cease to pray for you, and to ask that you may be filled with the knowledge of His will in all wisdom and spiritual understanding; that you may walk worthy of the Lord, fully pleasing Him, being fruitful in every good work and increasing in the knowledge of God; strengthened with all might, according to His glorious power, for all patience and longsuffering with joy; giving thanks to the Father who has qualified us to be partakers of the inheritance of the saints in the light. He has delivered us from the power of darkness and conveyed us into the kingdom of the Son of His love, in whom we have redemption through His blood, the forgiveness of sins (Colossians 1:9–14).*

Have you ever struggled in knowing how *precisely* to pray for another person, and especially how to pray for a person you may not know well? The apostle Paul gives us an outline! The prayer that he offered for the Colossians, a group of people whom he had never met but had only heard about through his colleagues Epaphras and Timothy, gives us a model for those things that we can pray with full assurance that we are praying God's will for another person. Note the six specifics of this prayer:

- *Filled with the knowledge of God's will—with all wisdom and spiritual understanding.* The apostle Paul does not say that the Colossians are already filled with this knowledge, but he does pray that they will be filled. He desires that they will know fully God's plan and purposes for their lives, not only the broad plan of obedience to God's commandments, but the specific daily plans and purposes that are revealed in an ongoing way by the Holy Spirit. He desires that they understand spiritual truth and know how to apply spiritual principles. He desires that they have an eternal perspective for all they do and say.

- *Walking worthy of the Lord, fully pleasing Him.* Those who walk "worthy of the Lord" are those who obey the Lord and seek to please Him in all of their actions and relationships.

- *Being fruitful in every good work.* To be "fruitful" means to be productive in ways that benefit or bless others. A "good work" is one that furthers God's kingdom.

- *Increasing in the knowledge of God.* We increase in our knowledge of God by what we read and study in God's Word, and also by what we gain as we develop a personal relationship with God through prayer and daily relating to Him.

- *Strengthened with all might, according to His glorious power, for all patience and longsuffering with joy.* It is the Holy Spirit who strengthens us to endure all situations that we encounter in life, and to do so with an inner wellspring of joy that is unrelated to outer circumstances.

- *Giving thanks to the Father.* Our thanksgiving is to flow from a sharp awareness of God's saving and delivering power—a clear understanding that we have been grasped from the clutches of the evil one, redeemed by the shed blood of Jesus, forgiven of our sins, and are now partakers of all the inheritance due the saints of God.

What a wonderful prayer this is to ask for others, including every member of your family *every day*! What a wonderful prayer to lift up for yourself!

Nothing about this prayer is contrary in the least to God's highest desires for a human being. God *wants* His beloved children to know His commands and purposes, to obey Him, to enjoy a fruitful life, to know Him better day by day, to be strong and joyful, and to be overflowing with gratitude for their salvation. It is as we live out the fullness of this prayer that we are in prime position to receive *all* of God's blessings.

Is there a particular phrase in this prayer that seems to stand out to you in a special way? Pray that *especially* for yourself and those you love . . . right now.

A
Application for Today

"Pray for me," the woman said to her Sunday school teacher after class one Sunday.

"What shall I pray for?" the teacher asked, noting the tears welling up in the woman's eyes.

"Just pray for ME," the woman said. "I'm a mess. Everything in my life is a mess."

The teacher felt a moment of panic and dismay. She didn't want to offend the woman standing before her by assuming that she had committed a terrible sin or that she was facing a life-threatening or life-changing situation. She truly wanted to pray in a way that would be both comforting and helpful. She quickly and silently prayed, "God, help me to pray in the right way. Give me the words to say."

The teacher then put her hands on the shoulders of the woman standing before her and prayed very slowly and with great intention, "May God's love and joy fill every crevice of your spirit, heart, mind, and body. May you know without any shadow of doubt that God is for you, not against you. May you come to understand His plans and purposes for you. May you grow in your relationship with God and become increasingly fruitful and strong. May you have thousands upon thousands of reasons to give God thanks and praise. I ask this in Jesus' name, Amen."

The woman gave her Sunday school teacher a big hug and said "thank you" and walked away. Several weeks later she came again to her teacher and said, "When you prayed for me I saw a picture in my mind. God was holding a big pitcher over my head and He began pouring love and joy into my life. It was slowly seeping down into every area of my heart that seemed to be cracked and dry—like a wonderful healing lotion. Every morning over the past few weeks I have awakened with a thought in my mind, 'thank God for His pouring love and joy into me.' I have been thanking God for His presence in my life every morning, and the more I have thanked Him, the more I have felt His presence with me all day long."

That morning, the Sunday school teacher prayed for HERSELF what she had prayed for her student. What an amazing thing to experience a "pouring in" of God's love and joy!

Do you need more of God's love and joy in your life today? Ask Him to pour Himself into your life in a way that is overflowing, healing, and comforting. Thank Him in an ongoing way for doing so!

S
Supplementary Scriptures to Consider

The apostle Paul's prayer for the Colossians was based upon a solid understanding of their faith in Christ Jesus:

> We give thanks to the God and Father of our Lord Jesus
> Christ, praying always for you, since we heard of your faith in
> Christ Jesus and of your love for all the saints; because of the
> hope which is laid up for you in heaven, of which you heard
> before in the word of the truth of the gospel, which has come

to you, as it has also in all the world, and is bringing forth
fruit, as it is also among you since the day you heard and
knew the grace of God in truth; as you also learned from
Epaphras, our dear fellow servant, who is a faithful minister of
Christ on your behalf, who also declared to us your love in the
Spirit (Colossians 1:3–8).

• How do your prayers for fellow believers in Christ Jesus differ from
prayers that you might pray for those who do not yet know Jesus as their
personal Savior?

• Is there a difference in the way you pray for fellow Christians who are
earnestly following Jesus as their Lord, and those who seem to have only
a nominal relationship with Jesus Christ?

The apostle Paul prayed this for the believers in Ephesus:

Peace to the brethren, and love with faith, from God the Father
and the Lord Jesus Christ. Grace be with all those
who love our Lord Jesus Christ in sincerity. Amen
(Ephesians 6:23–24).

- What does it mean to extend "peace" to a fellow believer? (Note that the word "peace," *shalom* in the Hebrew, refers to wholeness in spirit, soul, and body. *Shalom* is a concept directly related to both salvation and healing.)

- What does it mean to extend "love with faith" to a fellow believer?

- What does it mean to you to love the Lord Jesus Christ *in sincerity*? How might this type of love be related to grace, which is the working of God in a person's life?

The apostle Paul prayed this for Philemon:

> I thank my God, making mention of you always in my prayers, hearing of your love and faith which you have toward the Lord Jesus and toward all the saints, that the sharing of your faith may become effective by the acknowledgment of every good thing which is in you in Christ Jesus. For we have

great joy and consolation in your love, because the hearts of
the saints have been refreshed by you, brother (Philemon 4–7).

- Paul seems to give a basic definition for a Christian's "witness"—the
  sharing of a person's faith. He prays that Philemon's witness might
  become effective as Philemon acknowledges every good thing in his life
  that Christ Jesus has done or produced. What today would you note as the
  "good things" that Christ Jesus has done in or through your life?

- What does it mean for a person to "refresh" the hearts of fellow believers? How do we do this? In what ways might we do this better?

I
Introspection and Implications

1. How do you want others to pray for you?

2. To what extent are you willing to ask others to pray for you? To what extent are you willing to be vulnerable in expressing your weaknesses, flaws, failures, needs, or sins to another person?

3. Are you comfortable or uneasy when others note your good deeds or character traits as part of their prayers for you?

4. Do you ever feel challenged to "live up to" or to "manifest" to a greater extent what others have prayed for you?

5. Do you feel free to pray for others? What holds you back? In what ways do you feel limited in your ability to pray effectively for other people? What might you do to grow in your willingness or ability to pray for others?

C
Communicating the Good News

How might prayer along the lines of Colossians 1:9–14 become a part of your church as you seek to reach out to others in your community who do not know Jesus as their Savior?

- Does this prayer offer an outline for the way WE need to live as Christians who seek to give witness to the saving power of Jesus Christ?

- To what extent do we need to have greater knowledge—wisdom and spiritual understanding—about how to win the lost?

- In what ways do we need to be increasingly aware of our need to obey God as part of our Christian witness?

- In what ways do we need to grow in our knowledge of God in order to become better soul winners?

- In what ways do we need greater strength, patience, and joy as we witness to others?

Perhaps one of the most powerful witnesses we can make for Christ is to pour out our thanksgiving to God in appropriate verbal ways—to regularly express our reliance upon God and gratefulness for His work in our lives. In what ways might you incorporate more expressions of thanksgiving into your daily conversations?

LESSON #2

THE SUPREMACY OF CHRIST JESUS

Supremacy: a position of superiority or authority over all others

B
Bible Focus

> *He [Jesus] is the image of the invisible God, the firstborn over all creation. For by Him all things were created that are in heaven and that are on earth, visible and invisible, whether thrones or dominions or principalities or powers. All things were created through Him and for Him. And He is before all things, and in Him all things consist. And He is the head of the body, the church, who is the beginning, the firstborn from the dead, that in all things He may have the preeminence.*
>
> *For it pleased the Father that in Him all the fullness should dwell, and by Him to reconcile all things to Himself, by Him, whether things on earth or things in heaven, having made peace through the blood of His cross (Colossians 1:15–20).*

In this passage of Colossians, the apostle Paul was addressing the major heresy of his day: Gnosticism. While Gnosticism was rampant in the last half of the first century in the Greco-Roman world, the sad truth is that Gnosticism is *still* a major heresy in our world today.

We are so accustomed to living in a world that acknowledges the existence of one supreme God that we find it almost impossible to relate to the idea that at the time of the early church, *most* of the world believed in many gods. Every major culture had its own pantheon of gods and goddesses, some of them more powerful than others. The concept of one God, creator of *all*, was a decidedly Jewish concept, and through the Jews, a foundation stone of Christianity.

In the above passage, the apostle Paul affirmed the existence of God, creator and ruler of all things—both invisible and visible.

Most of the world at the time of Paul also believed that the suprametaphysical realm of the "spiritual" was separated from humanity and the physical world. The role of man was to serve as a butler to the gods— bringing them offerings of food and wine, and building them great temples in which to live. They believed that, if the gods accepted the service rendered to them, they might condescend to give man favorable crops, children, and business success.

In the above verses, the apostle Paul clearly contended that Jesus is both God and man—present at creation and also the supreme creation as God incarnate in human flesh. For most of the people who heard the gospel in the first century, this concept was earth-shattering and, at the same time, gloriously hope-filled.

A segment of the Greco-Roman society called Gnostics—literally "the intellectual ones"—further contended that God was spirit and good, but that all matter was evil and in opposition to God. They believed that a totally good God could not create matter directly, nor could God touch matter. They regarded the physical world as the result of a long series of emanations that God set into motion, until the final emanation was so distant from God that matter could be formed. To claim that Jesus—a human being living in a material, physical body—was divine, was unthinkable to the Gnostics. The Gnostics further believed that the way for a human being to have communication or reconciliation with God was to work his way intellectually back through the established series of emanations—each one having its own secret password and required level of knowledge. "Salvation" to them was an intellectual exercise that had nothing to do with the body—and certainly nothing to do with the body of Jesus Christ or His shed blood.

In the passage above, the apostle Paul clearly states that salvation is a matter of believing in the power of the shed blood of Jesus.

How, you may ask, is Gnosticism at work in our world today?

Countless people in the world today continue to believe in multiple gods and goddesses. This is not just limited to Hinduism and other eastern religions, which are increasing rather than decreasing in popularity in North America and European nations. Millions of people in the western world also believe in *themselves* as being gods and goddesses, or trust in human agencies and institutions to be god in their lives.

Countless people in our world today do not see any relationship between the spiritual world encountered on Sundays and the material or physical world which they face Monday through Saturday. They see God as distant and detached—a divine figurehead to be "served" through good works. They hope that their good works will satisfy a harsh and judgmental God, and be sufficient to earn them some degree of favor.

Countless people in our world today believe that, if they merely "think" enough good thoughts, they can know God. Others believe that only the "super spiritual" can ever truly know God personally.

Countless people in our world today believe that many other religions are equal to Christianity and that Jesus is not "supreme"— they believe that Jesus is not in a position of superiority or authority over all other "gods" or "religions."

How do you speak to those who might hold these opinions?

In what ways do you personally battle the pervasive perspective that man can earn his own salvation through good works and right attitudes—apart from the shed blood of Jesus?

A
Application for Today

"I like Jesus," a man said to his seatmate on an airline flight. "He was a good man. He taught some good things."

"But do you believe that He was God?" his seatmate asked.

"God? How could He be God? He was a man—a good man, but just a man."

"What do you do with the fact that Jesus spoke of Himself as being one with God—He was God incarnate, or God wrapped up in human flesh?"

The man shook his head and sighed. "I don't know what to do with that. Maybe I need to study spiritual things more."

"It isn't a matter of study. It is a matter of believing. The truth is—nobody can fully understand with his mind how Jesus could be God incarnate or be equal with God the creator as a member of the Trinity. There are some things that God requires for us simply to *believe*—to accept for no other reason than that He said so. In many ways, believing comes first, then understanding. That's opposite the way most people approach life—they must understand in order to believe. God's way is opposite. Believe . . . and then understand."

"But how can a person do that?" the first man asked. "It sounds like abandoning your mental ability."

"When you were a child, did your parents ever tell you to do something that you didn't understand?"

"Sure. Lots of things."

"You may not have understood why they were telling you to do certain things, but you likely have discovered the 'why' for some of their rules and words of advice since you became an adult."

"That's true."

"The same with God. Jesus said that He was the perfect manifestation of God the Father and that no person could come fully to God apart from believing in Him. Either Jesus was delusional and the biggest con artist who ever lived, or He was telling the truth. His life, and the lives of those who have believed in Him through the centuries, attest to the truth of His word. Even so, it is a step of faith to believe that Jesus was God and that the sacrificial death of Jesus on the cross provides the means for people to be forgiven of their sin and reconciled to God. Jesus said that 'whosoever believes' in Him would be forgiven and receive the gift of eternal life. It isn't a matter of understanding. It is a matter of believing."

If you had overheard this conversation, what would you have concluded?

What would you have said if the person next to you had turned to you and asked, "Do you believe what that guy is saying?"

S
Supplementary Scriptures to Consider

The apostle Paul recognized that what he was writing about Jesus was partially a "mystery":

> For I want you to know what a great conflict I have for you and those in Laodicea, and for as many as have not seen my face in the flesh, that their hearts may be encouraged, being knit together in love, and attaining to all riches of the full assurance of understanding, to the knowledge of the mystery of God, both of the Father and of Christ, in whom are hidden all the treasures of wisdom and knowledge (Colossians 2:1–3).

• Are you comfortable with the concept of "mystery" as it relates to certain aspects of your faith or your relationship with Christ Jesus?

• The apostle Paul also held out hope that the "knowledge of the mystery of God" could be understood at least to the degree of "full assurance." What does it mean to you to experience "full assurance of understanding" when it comes to the forgiveness of your sins, your reconciliation to God, and your future home in eternity?

- The apostle Paul stated that God the Father and God the Son hold all the "treasures of wisdom and knowledge," some of which remains hidden. What are some of the things that we who love Christ Jesus might never fully understand as long as we are on this earth?

The apostle Paul warned the Colossians that there would be those who would try to "cheat" them through philosophy and empty traditions:

> Beware lest anyone cheat you through philosophy and empty deceit, according to the tradition of men, according to the basic principles of the world, and not according to Christ. For in Him dwells all the fullness of the Godhead bodily; and you are complete in Him, who is the head of all principality and power (Colossians 2:8–10).

- To "cheat" is to short-change or to trick a person in some way that keeps the person from experiencing the fullness of what is owed him. Have you ever temporarily bought into a lie that kept you from experiencing the fullness of joy, peace, love, or blessing that God promised to you in His Word? What happened?

• One of the foremost lies foisted upon unsuspecting believers is that Jesus is not truly God and, therefore, He is not the "head" of all spiritual principalities and powers. This lie contends that people need to provide for their own salvation and deliverance because Jesus is insufficient— generally, the person who believes this lie feels a need to do certain good works in order to earn God's favor, healing, blessing, or deliverance because "mere" believing in Jesus isn't enough. Has anybody ever tried to convince you that you need to *add* something to your belief in Jesus in order to experience God's protection or provision? How did you respond?

The words of the apostle Paul to the Colossians seem to echo the opening verses of the Gospel of John:

> In the beginning was the Word, and the Word was with God,
> and the Word was God. He was in the beginning with God.
> All things were made through Him, and without Him nothing
> was made that was made…. And the Word became flesh and
> dwelt among us, and we beheld His glory as of the only
> begotten of the Father, full of grace and truth (John 1:1–3, 14).

• What similarities do you find between this passage and the passage of Colossians at the beginning of this chapter?

I
Introspection and Implications

1. Why do human beings have a seemingly inexplicable drive to try to "explain" God or understand God? In the ancient world, to have "knowledge" of something or someone gave a person a certain amount of control over that thing or person. Is our desire to try to "know" infinite God with our finite minds related to a desire to control God?

2. Why is the concept of "mystery" difficult for some Christians to embrace?

3. What have you come to understand about God since you first believed in Jesus as your Savior? Were these things that you understood before your conversion experience?

4. What is the difference between KNOWING God and knowing ABOUT God?

5. How do you explain the supremacy of Christ Jesus over all other "gods" or "religions"? Why is it important that you be able to give a good explanation about the supremacy of Christ?

C
Communicating the Good News

How much does a person need to know about Jesus or about God before he or she can be a good witness to others that Jesus is the Savior?

What does a person need to hear, or to know, about Jesus in order to accept Him as his or her Savior?

LESSON #3

THE LIMITATIONS OF LEGALISM

Legalism: the belief that deeds are required for salvation

B
Bible Focus

> Let no one judge you in food or in drink, or regarding a
> festival or a new moon or Sabbaths, which are a shadow of
> things to come, but the substance is of Christ. Let no one cheat
> you of your reward, taking delight in false humility and
> worship of angels, intruding into those things which he has
> not seen, vainly puffed up by his fleshly mind, and not holding
> fast to the Head, from whom all the body, nourished and knit
> together by joints and ligaments, grows with the increase that
> is from God.
>
> Therefore, if you died with Christ from the basic principles
> of the world, why, as though living in the world, do you
> subject yourselves to regulations—"Do not touch, do not taste,
> do not handle," which all concern things which perish with the
> using—according to the commandments and doctrines of
> men? These things indeed have an appearance of wisdom in
> self-imposed religion, false humility, and neglect of the body,
> but are of no value against the indulgence of the flesh (Colos-
> sians 2:16–23).

We do not know with certainty what *precisely* the false teachers were
saying to the Colossians, but the apostle Paul addresses three broad cate-
gories of false teaching that were common in the early church and are still
evident in our world today. These false teachings involved things that were
"added" to the gospel as practices vital for salvation or spiritual renewal
apart from simply believing in Jesus as the Christ.

*First, there were false teachings about what people should and should not
eat and drink.* Pagan religions nearly always involved ritual sacrifices of
food and drink offered to idols. This food and drink was sometimes offered
symbolically to a false god and then taken to a special market where it was
sold to the public. Those who purchased sacrificial meat and drink were
believed to "identify" with the idols and the false gods as they ate the same
food and drink offered to them. The apostle Paul taught plainly that regulations related to food and drink sold in the temple markets did not keep a
person from salvation, nor did the abstinence of consuming these items
contribute anything to a Christian's holiness.

*Second, there were false teachings about rites and rituals that needed to
be observed.* Some false teachers insisted that Christians keep all of the
Jewish feasts. Others insisted that Gentile Christians be circumcised as the
Jews were. Still others insisted that the flesh be denied or neglected in some

way—sometimes through prolonged fasting or even self-inflicted physical suffering. All of these rites and rituals were advocated for denying the flesh in order to give strength to the spirit. The apostle Paul stated clearly that these practices were not only unnecessary, but they created false humility and self-imposed religion, neither of which was helpful to a person's spiritual growth.

Third, there were false teachings about worshiping nature or worshiping angels. The influence of Gnosticism was evident in this. Those who taught the worship of angels believed that Jesus was just one of many intermediaries, or emanations, that required homage for salvation. Those who taught angel worship nearly always taught worship of the stars, and were strong advocates for astrology. The apostle Paul warned against worshiping anything or any one apart from Christ Jesus.

The sad truth is . . .

Many people today believe that how a person dresses or what a person consumes is a vital prerequisite for favor with God.

Many people believe that there are certain rituals that must be kept for salvation to be ensured.

Many people believe in the power of horoscopes or attempt to communicate with angels or spirit guides in order to become spiritually renewed or to be reconciled with God.

The apostle Paul would say to those who hold to such beliefs: "No, no, no! There are no *additions* to Christ Jesus. *Jesus is all sufficient and believing in Him is all that is required for salvation.*" The Bible tells us:

- What a person eats or drinks has nothing to do with redemption of a person's eternal spirit. Abstaining from certain foods or beverages may be prudent for health reasons, or be a wise consideration for a person's witness in leading others to the Lord or encouraging new believers, but such abstinence does not contribute to a person's salvation.

- Nothing needs to be observed apart from belief in Jesus as the Savior in order for a person to experience forgiveness of sin, reconciliation with God, and everlasting life.

- Nothing should be worshiped apart from Christ. No person should rely on any intermediary for access to God. No person should put his or her trust in any system related to the elements of the universe for favor with God.

Have you ever had someone tell you that there is something you need to do *in addition to* or *beyond* believing in Jesus in order for your sins to be forgiven or for you to be assured of everlasting life? They might not have said that in so many words, but at the same time this person could not imagine someone being a true Christian and *not* performing this action. If so, what did you do or say? What was the outcome?

If not, are you prepared for that possibility? Do you know what you would say and why?

A
Application for Today

Ten Commandments of Religion:

1. Thou shalt not eat meat, and especially thou shalt avoid pork and shellfish.
2. Thou shalt not wear fur or leather.
3. Thou shalt not drink anything other than pure water.
4. Thou shalt not wear make-up.
5. Thou shalt not wear slacks if thou art a woman.
6. Thou shalt not reveal the upper arms when in public.
7. Thou shalt not cut thy hair.
8. Thou shalt not be seen entering or leaving a place that known sinners frequent.
9. Thou shalt not have a bare or uncovered head when thou art in public view.
10. Thou shalt not smile in church.

Each of the above "commandments" continues to be taught by a major world religion or Christian denomination as a vital tenet for having a good relationship with God.

How do you respond to each of these commandments associated with religion?

Also reflect on these statements:

• Not all rules related to conduct violate a person's relationship with God.

• Some rules related to conduct fall into the category of "prudence" or "wisdom" when it comes to reflecting Christlike behavior or taking a stance against lewd or degenerative cultural norms.

• No rules such as these contribute to a person's salvation.

Do you agree or disagree with these statements?
On what basis?
To what end result?

S
Supplementary Scriptures to Consider

The Colossians apparently were being taught that circumcision was vital for new Gentile converts to Christ. The apostle Paul wrote about this:

> In Him you were also circumcised with the circumcision made without hands, by putting off the body of the sins of the flesh, by the circumcision of Christ, buried with Him in baptism, in which you also were raised with Him through faith in the working of God, who raised Him from the dead. And you, being dead in your trespasses and the uncircumcision of your flesh, He has made alive together with Him, having forgiven you all trespasses, having wiped out the handwriting of requirements that was against us, which was contrary to us. And He has taken it out of the way, having nailed it to the cross. Having disarmed principalities and powers, He made a public spectacle of them, triumphing over them in it (Colossians 2:11–15).

• Paul noted "circumcision made without hands"—a circumcision associated with a repentant heart and identification with the crucifixion and shed blood of Christ Jesus. Why is it important that a Christian identify with the death of Christ?

• What does it mean to you personally to "put off the body of the sins of the flesh?"

• Paul noted that the Colossians had received Christ and experienced salvation and renewal even while they were uncircumcised. How important is it to recognize that all people come to Christ *as sinners*?

• Paul presents this logic: We do not follow rules and regulations as a prerequisite for *receiving* Jesus Christ as our Savior or winning God's favor, so what could possibly be the benefit of following man-made rules and regulations as a means of *maintaining* favor with God or "holding on to" one's salvation? How do you respond to this statement of logic?

• Many false teachers contend that a person must keep certain rules and protocol in order to keep the devil away or to thwart evil spirits from attacking a person's life. Paul wrote: "Having disarmed principalities and powers, He made a public spectacle of them, triumphing over them in it." What do these words of Paul mean to you? If Christ defeated the devil and his minions at our salvation—without any works on our part—is there anything required for our spiritual protection apart from continuing to trust Christ to defeat the devil *after* our salvation?

Jesus warned against doctrines that were highly prescriptive when it came to behavior, but void of substance when it came to faith in God. (NOTE: Doctrine, by definition, is a body of ideas or principles that are taught to people as truth and as the basis for a belief or procedure.) Jesus said to His disciples:

"How is it you do not understand that I did not speak to you concerning bread?—but to beware of the leaven of the Pharisees and Sadducees." Then they understood that He did not tell them to beware of the leaven of bread, but of the doctrine of the Pharisees and Sadducees (Matthew 16:11–12).

Very specifically, Jesus said to the Pharisees about their "doctrine" related to righteousness before God—

"Woe to you, scribes and Pharisees, hypocrites! For you pay tithe of mint and anise and cummin, and have neglected the weightier matters of the law: justice and mercy and faith. These you ought to have done, without leaving the others undone. Blind guides, who strain out a gnat and swallow a camel!

"Woe to you, scribes and Pharisees, hypocrites! For you cleanse the outside of the cup and dish, but inside they are full of extortion and self-indulgence. Blind Pharisee, first cleanse the inside of the cup and dish, that the outside of them may be clean also.

"Woe to you, scribes and Pharisees, hypocrites! For you are like whitewashed tombs which indeed appear beautiful outwardly, but inside are full of dead men's bones and all uncleanness. Even so you also outwardly appear righteous to men, but inside you are full of hypocrisy and lawlessness.

"Woe to you, scribes and Pharisees, hypocrites! Because you build the tombs of the prophets and adorn the monuments of the righteous, and say, 'If we had lived in the days of our fathers, we would not have been partakers with them in the blood of the prophets.' Therefore you are witnesses against yourselves that you are sons of those who murdered the prophets (Matthew 23:23–31).

- The Pharisees and scribes equated their outward deeds with righteousness. They believed that keeping the prescribed laws, which went far beyond the Law of Moses, made a person righteous before God. To what practices or false doctrines do you believe Jesus might say "Woe!" today?

- Why do you believe it is easier for many people to "pay tithe of mint and anise and cummin" to the neglect of "the weightier matters of the law: justice and mercy and faith"?

I
Introspection and Implications

1. False teachers generally appeal to a person's desire to follow observable, measurable behaviors to gauge their spirituality. Why do you believe people are susceptible to this tactic?

2. In what ways is it valid to judge a person's outer behavior as being indicative of their inward spiritual state? What are the dangers in defining or evaluating a person's inner spiritual life according to outer behavior?

3. Respond to this statement: Jesus did not come to negate the Law, but to fulfill the Law (See Matthew 5:17). What does the phrase "fulfill the Law" mean? To what extent are we required to keep the Law today? How do we *fulfill* the Law in godly day-to-day behavior?

4. What is our proper relationship to the Law of Moses as believers in Christ Jesus?

5. What is the difference between being a law-keeper and being legalistic?

C
Communicating the Good News

Can you state in twenty-five words or less the difference between religion and a personal relationship with Christ Jesus?

Why is it important in our communication with the lost to place our emphasis on what Christ Jesus has done on their behalf, rather than on what they should do in order to receive Christ Jesus as their Savior?

What would you say to an unbeliever who claims, "I can't accept Jesus because there are just too many rules in religion that I can't keep"?

LESSON #4

PUTTING OFF THE OLD NATURE

Put off: remove from your life by an act of your will and faith

B
Bible Focus

> *If then you were raised with Christ, seek those things which are above, where Christ is, sitting at the right hand of God. Set your mind on things above, not on things on the earth. For you died and your life is hidden with Christ in God. When Christ who is our life appears, then you also will appear with Him in glory.*
>
> *Therefore put to death your members which are on the earth: fornication, uncleanness, passion, evil desire, and covetousness, which is idolatry. Because of these things the wrath of God is coming upon the sons of disobedience, in which you yourselves once walked when you lived in them.*
>
> *But now you yourselves are to put off all these: anger, wrath, malice, blasphemy, filthy language out of your mouth. Do not lie to one another, since you have put off the old man with his deeds, and have put on the new man who is renewed in knowledge according to the image of Him who created him, where there is neither Greek nor Jew, circumcised nor uncircumcised, barbarian, Sythian, slave nor free, but Christ is all and in all (Colossians 3:1–11).*

The gift of everlasting life is a wonderful treasure given to us when we accept Jesus as our personal Savior. What a glorious thing it is to anticipate our heavenly home and an eternal life in the service of God our King! Most Christians have great hope when it comes to heaven—they long to live in the perfection, beauty, and joy of heaven, including the splendors of their own heavenly mansion.

The apostle Paul encouraged the Colossians, however, not to wait for heaven to adopt heaven's "lifestyle." He said to them, in essence, "Start living now as you will live then. Live according to the behavioral codes and moral conduct of heaven NOW. You have not only been given everlasting life in the future, but you are called to live a holy, pure, abundant, and joyful live in the immediate present tense of your lives."

For the Christian, a godly life on this earth is like a training camp for the future lives that we will live in heaven. God desires the transformation of our lives *now*—He calls us to renewal, regeneration, and reconciliation, rather than continued conformity to the callousness, cold-heartedness, and sinfulness of the world.

The apostle Paul noted several behaviors that simply are not in keeping with the new character that the Holy Spirit makes possible for the believer. They include:

- *fornication and uncleanness.* Sexual sins are to be replaced with chastity and marital fidelity

- *passion and evil desire.* A drive toward fulfillment of lusts of all kinds is to be replaced with a bent toward those things that are pleasing to God

- *covetousness.* The desire for more power and possessions is to be replaced with generosity and service

- *anger and wrath.* Both the sudden blaze of temper and the slow-burning anger that seethes inside a person are to be replaced with expressions of kindness

- *malice.* Vicious hatred is to be replaced with love

- *blasphemy.* Insulting language against God is to be replaced with praise

- *filthy language.* Obscenities are to be replaced with words that encourage, inspire, and edify

- *lying.* Dealing in deception and believing falsehoods are to be replaced with truth

- *prejudice against other believers.* Distinctions according to class and race are to be replaced with acceptance of other believers to the point that we do not even see their race or class, but only that they are "in Christ" alongside us

All of these aspects of behavior—related to thought, word, and deed—are subject to human will. God's promise is always that as we exert our will to do His will, He will give us the power to make positive changes. We *can* put off old mental, emotional, and behavioral patterns. We *can* cast aside the nature that is contrary to the way that we will think, speak, and act in heaven! The Holy Spirit will help us do this—He is our ever-present counselor and helper as we prepare ourselves for life in heaven one day.

In casting off the old nature, the main question we must ask ourselves often is, "In what ways do I exhibit behaviors, ideas, emotions, or speech that Jesus did not exhibit? In what ways am I living in a way that He did not live?"

Those are sobering questions that can only be answered personally and must be answered honestly by each one of us. Any behavior that is not Christlike is a behavior that we are wise to change.

A
Application for Today

The two women stood before the walk-in closet and sighed deeply.

"Wow, you have a lot of stuff," one woman said.

"Too much. And none of it is organized and half of it doesn't fit any more. I really need to clear things out," said the closet owner.

"Well, first," the closet-organizing friend suggested, "we should get rid of everything that isn't your size."

"But what if I regain the weight I've lost and need some of those outfits?" the closet owner said.

"No! You are not going to regain the weight you've lost. We're getting rid of everything that is now too big for you!"

"Shouldn't I take some of those garments to be altered?"

"No, you can buy new things for about the same price as good alteration. Those old clothes will remind you of days when you were overweight. Consider them your fat clothes—lose them like you lost the fat!"

The two women worked for a couple of hours sorting out clothes by size and by noon they had reduced the contents of the clothes closet in half. Shoes that were well-worn or outdated were also put in the "giveaway" box.

A few items that fit, but which had spots that could not be removed, were tossed into a "rags" basket.

The friend then said, "Now, we need to get rid of a few things that don't fit your new life. Since you accepted Jesus as your Savior, you don't go to clubs and come home at two in the morning. You need to get rid of those clothes that were your clubbing clothes." Several more outfits hit the give-away box.

At the end of the day, the closet was cleared, items were taken to a homeless shelter, and the two celebrated their accomplishment: a closet filled with items that both could and should be worn.

What behaviors, thoughts, and attitudes no longer "fit" you as a person who has accepted Jesus as your Savior and is seeking to follow Him daily as your Lord?

What needs to be cleared out of your spiritual-life closet so that you truly might reflect Christ to your world?

S
Supplementary Scriptures to Consider

Paul wrote to the Ephesians:

> But you have not so learned Christ, if indeed you have heard Him and have been taught by Him, as the truth is in Jesus, that you put off, concerning your former conduct, the old man which grows corrupt according to the deceitful lusts, and be renewed in the spirit of your mind, and that you put on the new man which was created according to God, in true righteousness and holiness.
>
> Therefore, putting away lying, "let each one of you speak truth with his neighbor," for we are members of one another. "Be angry, and do not sin"; do not let the sun go down on your wrath, nor give place to the devil. Let him who stole steal no longer, but rather let him labor, working with his hands what is good, that he may have something to give him who has need. Let no corrupt word proceed out of your mouth, but what is good for necessary edification, that it may impart grace to the hearers. And do not grieve the Holy Spirit of God, by whom you were sealed for the day of redemption. Let all bitterness, wrath, anger, clamor, and evil speaking be put away from you, with all malice. And be kind to one another, tenderhearted, forgiving one another, even as God in Christ forgave you (Ephesians 4:20–33).

• What has been the most difficult aspect of your "old nature" to give up or put off?

- As you look back over your life in Christ Jesus, can you see a progression in behaviors, words, and thoughts that the Holy Spirit led you to discard or exchange?

- What or who helped you the most as you directed your will toward putting off old ungodly behaviors and putting on new godly behaviors?

- What does it mean to "grieve" the Holy Spirit? How can we *not* grieve the Holy Spirit?

Jesus taught His disciples to pray:

> "Your kingdom come.
> Your will be done
> On earth as it is in heaven" (Matthew 6:10).

- How do you envision that you will think or feel emotionally in heaven one day? How do you think you will speak to those you encounter in heaven? How will you act?

- To what extent can we live on earth according to heaven's rules and protocol? What hinders us from living completely in accordance with the way that things function in heaven?

I
Introspection and Implications

1. Where do you get knowledge about heaven and the way that things "function" for those who live in heaven?

2. How difficult is it for you to "seek those things which are above" rather than become embroiled in the "way that things are here on earth"? What do you do, personally, to focus on those things that are "highest and best" according to God's will?

3. The apostle Paul said, "Set your mind on things above, not on things on the earth." How do we do this? How can we keep our mind on heavenly things and still do our jobs and fulfill our responsibilities on earth? How can we become heavenly-minded and still be of "earthly good" to our families and friends?

4. Jesus is our role model for godly character and behavior. How can we keep Jesus in the forefront of our thinking on a daily basis so that we might "copy" the ways in which He thought, spoke, and acted?

C
Communicating the Good News

Many people believe that they must change their lives before they can accept Jesus as their Savior. They assume that they must "get good" before they can "get God." What would you say to a person who expressed this belief to you?

The good news of the gospel is that God changes our sin nature so that we no longer are in bondage to sin—in other words, we no longer have an overriding compulsion to sin. Rather, the Spirit of God frees us so that we might have an overwhelming desire to do what is right in God's eyes. To what extent and in what ways can we convey to unbelievers that they can trust God to help them make changes in their lives?

LESSON #5

PUTTING ON A NEW NATURE

Holy: dedicated or set apart for God's purposes, totally devoted to the service of God

B
Bible Focus

> As the elect of God, holy and beloved, put on tender
> mercies, kindness, humility, meekness, longsuffering; bearing
> with one another, and forgiving one another, if anyone has a
> complaint against another; even as Christ forgave you, so you
> also must do. But above all these things put on love, which is
> the bond of perfection. And let the peace of God rule in your
> hearts, to which also you were called in one body; and be
> thankful. Let the word of Christ dwell in you richly in all
> wisdom, teaching and admonishing one another in psalms and
> hymns and spiritual songs, singing with grace in your hearts
> to the Lord. And whatever you do in word or deed, do all in
> the name of the Lord Jesus, giving thanks to God the Father
> through Him (Colossians 3:12–17).

Just as it is within our human will to "put off" old behaviors, so we have the
God-given ability to "put on" a new lifestyle. The Holy Spirit gives us His
POWER to go along with our WILL so that we truly have godly *WILL
POWER*. God's call to us is to put on

- *tender mercies and kindness.* Pitifully few provisions were made in the
  ancient world for the sick, maimed, aged, mentally ill, or mentally
  impaired. Paul called upon the church to extend mercy to those in need
  and to show kindness in the face of indignity and injustice. The need for
  mercy and kindness is equally prevalent in our world today.

- *humility and meekness.* To be humble is to be aware that man is the
  "created," God is the Creator. In every way that man's power, wisdom,
  presence, or ability to love and forgive is finite and tends to be condi-
  tional, God is infinite and His love is unconditional. To be meek is to
  yield to God's directives.

- *longsuffering and bearing with one another.* Our human patience is to be
  a reflection of God's patience. To the degree that God "suffers long" on
  our behalf, we are to be patient with others.

- *forgiveness.* Forgiveness is releasing the hurts of our hearts so that God
  might strengthen us and restore us to wholeness.

- *love.* This is love that mirrors God's love, which always believes in the
  best in another person.

• *thankfulness.* We are called to have an ongoing attitude of gratitude and to voice thanksgiving for all that God has done and given in the past, is doing and giving in the present, and promises to do and to give in the future.

None of these attributes of Christian virtue is *easy* to "put on"—but all of these attributes are reflective of Jesus' nature and character. He is our role model. The Spirit dwells within us to produce the character traits of Christ Jesus if we are willing both to ask and to pursue these virtues. The apostle Paul makes it clear that we are chosen (elect), in a unique position to receive God's favor (holy), and love (beloved). In other words, we are capable of manifesting the superb qualities described in this passage, only we must be willing to ask the Holy Spirit to produce His character within us and to help us make the right attitudinal and behavioral choices in every situation or circumstance that we encounter.

The apostle Paul called the Colossians to three specific actions:

• *The Word of God dwelling in them "richly in all wisdom."* Before we can live out the truth of God's Word in our daily lives, we must *know* God's Word. There is no substitute for daily reading and studying the Scriptures. A knowledge of God's Word is a prerequisite for godly wisdom.

• *Teaching and admonishing one another in "psalms and hymns and spiritual songs."* We are to help one another "put on" Christ. Teaching enlightens the mind. Admonishing redirects the will and heart of a person. The best vehicle for admonishing others is to speak to them in language that touches their innermost emotions.

• *Doing all things in the name of the Lord Jesus.* To do things "in the name of" another person is to do things "in their nature"—thinking, speaking, and acting as the other person would act, and in so doing, taking on their identity and character. This is our goal!

What is it that you are feeling a need to "put on" today?

A
Application for Today

There's something about a song that touches the human heart. We all know that a song can inspire us to greater heights and instill courage, faith, or patriotism in us. A song is capable of bringing a tear to our eye, comforting us when we are feeling low, or mollifying our anger or frustration. A song can set our toes tapping when we feel discouraged, cause us to smile in remembrance of a happy time, or cause overflowing joy and praise to well up in our souls.

The Jewish people throughout their history have been quick to burst into song. A number of key passages in the Old Testament were "songs." The word "psalm" means "song." The prophetic words of Deborah and other prophets were often expressed in song. A song such as that sung by Mary, the mother of Jesus, was usually created for each child as an expression of the hopes of a mother for her baby.

The apostle Paul wrote to the Colossians that they were to admonish one another in "psalms and hymns and spiritual songs." Admonishment is often difficult to convey and not easy to receive because it is a word to us that we should change our behavior—admonishment provides a "wake-up" call that we are doing something that we should stop doing, start doing something that we presently aren't doing, or change our behavior or tactics in some way. Admonishment in song goes straight to the heart, bypassing all *mental* excuses, justifications, arguments, and resistance. Admonishment that is couched in song is often easier to express and easier to "hear" than admonishment that is spoken without music.

Reflect on your answers to these questions:

- What are some of your favorite songs? Secular songs? Religious songs? Why?

- Do you ever sing a unique "spiritual song" to the Lord—in praise, or as part of your prayers? What spiritual benefit do you receive from singing in this way?

- Do you ever sing as a way of releasing emotions—perhaps singing when you are fearful or anxious, singing when you are sad, or singing when you are very happy?

- How would you go about admonishing another person in song?

S
Supplementary Scriptures to Consider

The apostle Paul was not the only one to regard Christians as God's "elect" with a unique set of character traits. We read in the first letter of Peter:

> You are a chosen generation, a royal priesthood, a holy nation,
> His own special people, that you may proclaim the praises of

Him who called you out of darkness into His marvelous light,
who once were not a people but are now the people of God,
who had not obtained mercy but now have obtained mercy
(1 Peter 2:9–11).

• What does it mean to you to be part of God's "elect"—a "chosen" genera-
tion?

• What does it mean to you to be considered by God to be "holy" (which
means cleansed and separated for God's use)?

• What does Peter state as the *reason* that we are a special people of God?

Part of the passage cited at the beginning of this lesson is expressed in
another version of the Bible this way:

"Clothe yourselves with love which is the perfect bond; and
let the peace of God be the decider of all things within your
hearts, for it is to that peace you were called, so that you

might be united in one body" (Colossians 3:14–15, William
Barclay translation).

- Paul notes that love is what "binds" us to one another in Christ. Can you
  cite an example of this in your personal life? Is love the "binding force"
  in your church? How so? In what ways might this bond be strengthened
  in your personal life? In your church?

- The "deciding" rule for any situation, according to this passage of Scripture, is "does it produce God's peace, which is wholeness?" Consider a
  situation facing you, your family, or your church. What are the possible
  solutions that fit this deciding rule?

- Paul notes that Christians are "called" to peace so that they may be united
  in one body. Why is it important for us to be in communion and union
  with other believers? How does wholeness, or peace (*shalom*), unite us
  into one body in Christ Jesus?

I
Introspection and Implications

1. As human beings, we tend to be egocentric from our birth—subconsciously, if not consciously, we are prone to ask, "What's in it for me?" The traits that Paul calls upon the Colossians to "put on" are traits that are not only related to our personal self and relationship with God, but they are also characteristics manifested in our relationships with other people. Look again at these character traits and ask about each one, "How might MORE of this particular character trait affect my relationship with _____ ?" Think of specific individuals as you evaluate each trait:

   • tender mercies and kindness

   • humility and meekness

   • longsuffering and bearing with one another

   • forgiveness

   • love

   • thankfulness

2. Reflect upon the life and ministry of Jesus. Think of ways in which Jesus modeled these character traits:

   • tender mercies and kindness

   • humility and meekness

   • longsuffering and bearing with one another

   • forgiveness

   • love

   • thankfulness

3. What is it that you feel responsible for teaching others?

4. Have you ever "admonished" another person? What was the outcome?

5. Have you ever been "admonished" by someone? How did you respond?

C
Communicating the Good News

What do you believe to be the role or benefit of music in reaching out to unbelievers?

How might each of the traits identified by the apostle Paul in this passage relate to evangelism?

- expressing tender mercies and kindness

- acting in humility and meekness

- showing patience

- freely forgiving

- expressing God's love

- giving thanks

Lesson #6

THE CHRISTIAN HOME

Heartily: in a sincere, enthusiastic, full and complete way

B
Bible Focus

> Wives, submit to your own husbands, as is fitting in the Lord.
>
> Husbands, love your wives and do not be bitter toward them.
>
> Children, obey your parents in all things, for this is well pleasing to the Lord.
>
> Fathers, do not provoke your children, lest they become discouraged.
>
> . . . And whatever you do, do it heartily, as to the Lord and not to men, knowing that from the Lord you will receive the reward of the inheritance; for you serve the Lord Christ. But he who does wrong will be repaid for what he has done, and there is no partiality (Colossians 3:18–21, 23–25).

So many people today describe the family of their childhood as having been "dysfunctional." We seem to have woefully few role models of a functional family in our society! In just a few sentences, however, the apostle Paul gave the skeletal outline for what might have been a complete course in "Functional Family 101."

At the heart of this passage is a very strong concept that runs throughout the Bible and Jewish history: *reciprocity in obligations*. This concept is rooted in an understanding that in any relationship between two people, each party to the relationship has a responsibility and obligation to the other party. For the relationship to be sound and to function smoothly, both parties must fulfill their obligations.

In a marriage, Paul teaches submission of a wife to a husband, and love of a husband for a wife. To submit is to show respect and to yield in decision-making. To love is to show affection and to provide protection and provision. But just look at how wonderfully these two "obligations" work in reciprocity! It is EASY for a husband to show affection and be a willing provider and protector of a wife who respects him and yields to his decision-making. It is EASY for a wife to respect and yield to a husband who is affectionate toward her and who protects and provides for her as his first priority. "Reciprocity in obligation" produces an atmosphere that is delightful—void of bitterness, resentment, and rejection. The marriage functions smoothly and is beneficial to both parties.

The same holds true for the parent-child relationship. To obey is to follow the instructions or commands of a superior authority. To refrain from "provoking" means to keep from pushing a child into rebellion. What causes a child to rebel against parental authority? Usually rebellion arises when a child believes that the parent has been unjust, overly critical, excessively demanding, or absent emotionally (which causes feelings of rejection). What does reciprocity in obligation produce? A child finds it EASY to obey a parent who freely expresses love and value, gives direction that is clear, helps the child set realistic goals in keeping with the child's natural traits and abilities, and who offers ongoing praise and encouragement for the child's successes. A parent finds it EASY to offer guidance, express emotion, and encourage a child who is obedient. "Reciprocity in obligation" produces an atmosphere in the home that is pleasant and positive—void of angry outbursts or sullen silence. The parent-child relationship functions smoothly and is beneficial to both parent and child.

Converse with your spouse today. Talk to your child today. If you have experienced a lack of "reciprocity in obligation," admit your own failings, ask for forgiveness, and ask the other person to join you in making a new beginning in the way that you relate to each other. Recognize openly that the alternative is for each offending person to be chastised by the Lord and for the family to fail. Also, be encouraged that, if you uphold *your* role in the marriage, or as a parent or child, the Lord will find a way to reward you.

A
Application for Today

"How can she stay in that marriage?"

"How can he put up with her as a wife?"

"How can I endure another day of this marital misery?"

"How much more can I take from my rebellious child?"

These are questions that we often ask silently, and sometimes openly, about relationships that seem to have gone amuck and become painful or problematic, sometimes *exceedingly* painful and problematic.

The apostle Paul gives a clue to *enduring* in a difficult relationship, and brilliant counsel about how to *avoid* the breakdown of a marriage or parenting relationship. He said, "Whatever you do, do it heartily, as to the Lord and not to men."

This means treating the other person as if that individual were Christ Jesus Himself.

A woman once said: "My husband likes a very clean and neat house. I grew up in a home where housekeeping didn't matter all that much, but out of respect for my husband, I decided when I married him that I would do my best to keep the house in the way he liked it. It was hard work. I didn't like it. But an older friend finally advised me, 'Clean your house as if you were cleaning it for Jesus to come visit you.' That made all the difference."

A man once said, "My wife has this thing about lamps and pillows. She likes expensive lamps and is always changing the pillows on the sofa and chairs in various rooms. I think it's a waste of money but I finally decided, 'She's trying to make a nice home for me.' I set aside a little money now and then say, 'Honey, why don't you go buy something you'd like.' It's always a lamp or some pillows. One Sunday our pastor said, 'When you give something to your wife that she wants, even though you don't necessarily want it, you are showing love and that pleases God.' That made it even easier to come up with that lamps-and-pillows money."

What difference might be made in your home if you did things for your spouse, or treated your children, in a way that was "as to the Lord"?

S
Supplementary Scriptures to Consider

The apostle Paul wrote very similar parenting advice to the Ephesians:

> Children, obey your parents in the Lord, for this is right. Honor your father and mother," which is the first commandment with promise: "that it may be well with you and you may live long on the earth."
>
> And you, fathers, do not provoke your children to wrath, but bring them up in the training and admonition of the Lord (Ephesians 6:1–4).

• To "honor" is to respect. How, in very practical terms, can a child honor a mother and father? What about after the child reaches adulthood? What about those cases in which the parent may have been neglectful or abusive?

• What does it mean to bring up a child in the "training and admonition of the Lord"? How can this be done in a way that does not provoke wrath in a child? (NOTE: "wrath" is seething, ongoing anger.)

The apostle Paul wrote this advice to husbands and wives in his letter to the Ephesians:

> "Wives, submit to your own husband, as to the Lord. For the husband is head of the wife, as also Christ is head of the church; and He is the Savior of the body. Therefore, just as the church is subject to Christ, so let the wives be to their own husbands in everything."
>
> "Husbands, love your wives, just as Christ also loved the church and gave Himself for her, that He might sanctify and cleanse her with the washing of water by the word, that He might present her to Himself a glorious church, not having spot or wrinkle or any such thing, but that she should be holy and without blemish. So husbands ought to love their own wives as their own bodies; he who loves his wife loves himself. For no one ever hated his own flesh, but nourishes and cherishes it, just as the Lord does the church. For we are members of His body, of His flesh and of His bones. "For this reason a man shall leave his father and mother an be joined to his wife, and the two shall become one flesh." This is a great mystery, but I speak concerning Christ and the church. Nevertheless let each one of you in particular so love his own wife as himself, and let the wife see that she respects her husband" (Ephesians 5:22–33).

- What makes a wife *willing* to submit to her own husband?

- What makes a husband *willing* to love his wife?

- What causes a woman to "respect" her husband?

- What motivates a man to love his wife "as himself"?

I

Introspection and Implications

1. What do you believe are the foremost challenges that husbands and wives face in today's world? What do you believe are the most important things that a husband or wife might do to strengthen their marriage?

2. What do you believe are the foremost challenges that parents face in today's world? What do you believe are the most important things that parents might do to strengthen their relationship with their children?

C
Communicating the Good News

How is God best presented as a loving Father to a person who had a highly flawed earthly father?

In some churches, evangelism is presented as a "family challenge"—an entire family is encouraged to work together to witness to unbelieving neighbors and the families of those with whom they work or attend school. What unique opportunities for evangelism might your family have in your community?

HOW TO TREAT THOSE WHO SERVE YOU OR RULE OVER YOU

Bondservant: a serf or slave

B
Bible Focus

> *Though I might be very bold in Christ to command you what is fitting, yet for love's sake I rather appeal to you—being such a one as Paul, the aged, and now also a prisoner of Jesus Christ—I appeal to you for my son Onesimus, whom I have begotten while in my chains, who once was unprofitable to you, but now is profitable to you and to me.*
>
> *I am sending him back. You therefore receive him, that is, my own heart, whom I wished to keep with me, that on your behalf he might minister to me in my chains for the gospel. But without your consent I wanted to do nothing that your good deed might not be by compulsion, as it were, but voluntary.*
>
> *For perhaps he departed for a while for this purpose, that you might receive him forever, no longer as a slave but more than a slave—a beloved brother, especially to me but how much more to you, both in the flesh and in the Lord.*
>
> *If then you count me as a partner, receive him as you would me (Philemon 8-17).*

Slavery was common in the time of the apostle Paul, and many Christians in the first-century church were either slaves or slave owners. Slaves were not only kept by Greeks and Romans. It was entirely possible under Jewish law for a Jew to submit himself to another Jew as a "bondservant" in order to pay off a debt, or in order to be helped financially for a period of time. The primary difference between Jewish bondservants and Greek-Roman slaves was that Jewish bondservants were allowed their freedom after seven years of service, and the relationship between Jewish bondservants and their masters tended to be mutual, at least to a degree—one person seeking financial and material help and protection, and the other willing to provide it. From a Jewish perspective in the first century, slavery was not considered to be necessarily a bad thing—the relationship between master and slave could be mutually advantageous.

In Philemon, the one-chapter book of the New Testament, the apostle Paul is writing to a man named Philemon about one of his runaway slaves named Onesimus. Most biblical scholars believe that Philemon lived in Colosse. Paul wrote his letters to the Colossians and also the Ephesians, while he was in prison in Rome—where he apparently met and led Onesimus to faith in Christ Jesus.

Paul made two statements in the passage above that would have been stunning to those who read his letter.

First, Paul stated that Onesimus was once "unprofitable" to Philemon, but is now profitable to him and to Paul. This is something of a play on words since the name Onesimus means "profitable." As a slave, Onesimus no doubt was rebellious in his heart and attitude long before he ran away from Colosse to Rome. This fact relates directly to many employees today who hate their jobs and despise their bosses. Resentful, bitter, or disenchanted employees, or slaves, never give full energy, loyalty, or maximum creativity totheir work. Often, such employees foment negative morale among other employees. After coming to Christ, however, Onesimus truly had a servant's *heart*. Paul had been the recipient of his generosity and loyalty, to the point that he expressed a desire to keep Onesimus by his side.

Second, Paul noted that Onesimus' running away may have been part of God's greater plan for both Onesimus and Philemon. Paul wrote, "Perhaps he departed for a while for this purpose, that you might receive him forever." Onesimus had found Christ Jesus in Rome. And now, Philemon was going to be given an opportunity to be a genuine brother in Christ to Onesimus and learn what it meant to forgive fully and embrace a former slave as a Christian brother. Together, Philemon and Onesimus had the potential to be a tremendous witness to the church in Colosse, and to all believers and nonbelievers who heard their story. They had the opportunity to be a shining example of true reconciliation in Christ Jesus. Indeed, Philemon and Onesimus continue to influence us today *because* Onesimus first ran away. We are wise to recognize that *all* things that happen to us, and in our relationships, can be used by God for our eternal *and* earthly good if we will seek God's highest plans and purposes in the circumstances of our lives.

Third, Paul desired that Philemon receive Onesimus back into his household as "more than a slave—a beloved brother." One of the amazing facts of this story is that Onesimus was willing to return to Philemon. He trusted God to work in his life, even if it meant becoming a slave once again. There was nothing that *required* Philemon to receive him back, or to treat him well. There was nothing that ensured that Philemon would take Paul's words to heart. The challenge that Paul set before Philemon, however, was one that reflected the true heart of God. It became the challenge set before all slave owners, and today it is the challenge set before all employers, supervisors, or leaders: Treat ALL Christians who serve you in any capacity as MORE than servants. Treat them as beloved brothers and sisters.

In what ways does the story of Onesimus challenge you to be a better employee, worker, committee member, church member, or volunteer in the service of others?

In what ways does Paul's admonition to Philemon challenge you to be a better employer, supervisor, or leader of others?

A
Application for Today

As strange as it may seem to us today, slavery was an acceptable part of cultures around the world until the mid-nineteenth century. Largely through the sustained and focused efforts of William Wilberforce and his friend, English Prime Minister William Pitt, slavery was abolished in England, and subsequently, the United States. Even so, "forced labor" still exists in many parts of the world on a widespread basis.

Some have criticized the apostle Paul for not calling upon the Christians to rise up against slavery and seek its abolition in the first century. To have done so, however, would have been to create widespread anarchy and harsh retaliation upon the Christian community—precisely at the time when the church was being established. Rather than incite cultural revolution outwardly, Paul called upon the church to pray for those in authority that there might be peace—not only that Christians might live in peace and avoid persecution, but so evangelism efforts might flourish.

Rather than seek to transform the SYSTEM, the apostle Paul sought to inspire transformation in the LIVES of men and women who lived within the system. His teachings were a radical idea to those who encountered them: masters were admonished to *love* their slaves, whom they previously had regarded as property. Slaves were admonished to respect their masters and give their utmost and highest efforts to them.

In the twentieth century, communism held many in its grip as a political SYSTEM. Many Christian leaders around the world adopted Paul's stance—they encouraged the believers in communist nations to pray for their leaders, obey them, and pursue transformation of human lives and relationships within the system, rather than seek to overthrow the system. The result was that underground churches flourished.

The change required to revamp entire political, cultural, or religious SYSTEMS can take decades, even centuries. The change involved in altering RELATIONSHIPS and individual HUMAN LIVES within any given system can occur in a heartbeat.

Is there a system today that you believe needs to be overhauled from the ground up?

What value do you perceive in diligent and concerted prayer for those in leadership?

How might you seek to inspire transformation in the lives of those who are caught up in the system?

S
Supplementary Scriptures to Consider

Even as the apostle Paul wrote to a slave owner named Philemon, he wrote this to the church in Colosse:

> Masters, give your bondservants what is just and fair, knowing that you also have a Master in heaven (Colossians 4:1).

- How does our thinking change when we recognize fully that the way we treat others is recognized—and either rewarded or chastised—by our Heavenly Father?

- In a system in which people are perceived as property or "things"—or in our case today, roles, numbers, or job descriptions—what are the challenges involved in doing what is just and fair? As long as we see people as "objects," how generous toward people are we likely to be?

- How would you apply this directive of Paul to employers, supervisors, and other types of leaders in today's work force?

The apostle Paul said this to those who were bondservants in the church:

> Bondservants, obey in all things your masters according to the flesh, not with eyeservice, as men-pleasers, but in sincerity of heart, fearing God (Colossians 3:22).

- How do you describe the difference between giving "eyeservice" as "men-pleasers," and acting with genuine sincerity of heart?

- Note that Paul admonished those who were bondservants to obey their masters "according to the flesh." Certainly this precluded a bondservant ever obeying a master who attempted to coerce a bondservant into false beliefs or denial of Jesus Christ as Savior. What is the proper position to take if someone in authority over you demands that you violate the commandments of God, or deny Jesus as your Savior and Lord?

- How would you apply this directive of Paul to employees and all other "followers" in task-related relationships?

Paul gave the same advice to bondservants that he offered to family relationships: act "as unto the Lord."

> Bondservants, be obedient to those who are your masters according to the flesh, with fear and trembling, in sincerity of heart, as to Christ; not with eyeservice, as men-pleasers, but as bondservants of Christ, doing the will of God from the heart, with goodwill doing service, as to the Lord, and not to men, knowing that whatever good anyone does, he will receive the same from the Lord, whether he is a slave or free (Ephesians 6:5–8).

• Identify specific ways in which you are a bondservant of Christ?

• In what ways do you envision these words having great impact upon, and being a source of encouragement to those who were slaves in the early church: "Knowing that whatever good anyone does, he will receive the same from the Lord, whether he is a slave or free"? In what ways do these words encourage you?

Paul specifically admonished the masters in Ephesus to understand that they had no "favored status" before God:

> And you, masters, do the same things to them, giving up threatening, knowing that your own Master also is in heaven, and there is no partiality with Him (Ephesians 6:9).

• Is anything good ever gained—in the long run—from threatening another person?

• What do you think leads certain people to believe that they have "favored status" before God, that the normal commandments and rules of Scripture do not apply to them personally? Or, to conclude that they are more deserving of God's rewards and blessings than others?

I
Introspection and Implications

1. In what ways does the Book of Philemon challenge you regarding your leader-follower relationships? If you are an employer or leader, how might you do a better job? If you are an employee or follower, how might you serve the Lord where you work?

2. Refer to the previous lesson on "reciprocity of obligation." In what ways is it easier to obey a person in authority over you—and to give service from the heart—if that person is just, fair, and loving toward you? In what ways is it easier to lead people who do not have a rebellious attitude and who give their best effort and talent to the tasks assigned them?

3. Is there a relationship at work that you'd like to see transformed into a godly friendship? How might you go about pursuing that transformation?

4. Do you ever feel like a "slave"—at work, at home, even in your church work? How do the book of Philemon and Paul's letter to the Colossians speak to you?

5. Do you ever grow weary of being a leader? How do the book of Philemon and related passages in Colossians encourage you?

6. Nearly every person in modern society has a mix of "slave" and "master" roles that he or she fills. How might a person move with maximum graciousness from one role to the next?

C
Communicating the Good News

How important are manifestations of loving, fair, and just leadership to evangelism?

What happens in any effort to win the lost when a "master" becomes too harsh, too demanding, or too strident in his or her demands?

NOTES TO LEADERS
OF SMALL GROUPS

A s the leader of a small discussion group, think of yourself as a facilitator
with three main roles:

- Get the discussion started

- Involve every person in the group

- Encourage an open, candid discussion that remains focused on the Bible

You certainly don't need to be the person with all the answers! In truth,
much of your role is to ask questions, such as:

- What impacted you most in this lesson?

- What part of the lesson did you find troubling?

- What part of the lesson was encouraging or insightful?

- What part of the lesson would you like to explore further?

Express to the group at the outset of your study that your goal as a group
is to gain new insights into God's Word—this is not the forum for defending
a point of doctrine or a theological opinion. Stay focused on what God's
Word says and means. The purpose of the study is also to share insights of
how to apply God's Word to everyday life. *Every* person in the group can
and should contribute—the collective wisdom that flows from Bible-focused
discussion is often very rich and deep.

Seek to create an environment in which every member of the group feels free to ask questions of other members to gain greater understanding. Encourage group members to voice their appreciation to one another for new insights gained, and to be supportive of one another personally. Take the lead in doing this. Genuinely appreciate and value the contributions each person makes.

You may want to begin each study by having one or more members of the group read through the section provided under "Bible Focus." Ask the group specifically if it desires to discuss any of the questions under the "Application for Today" section, the "Supplemental Scriptures to Consider" section, and the "Introspection and Implications" and "Communicating the Good News" section. You do not need to come to a definitive conclusion or consensus about any question asked in this study. Rather, encourage your group if it does not have a satisfactory Bible-based answer to a question that the group engage in further asking, seeking, and knocking strategies to discover the answers! Remember the words of Jesus: "Ask, and it will be given to you; seek, and you will find; knock, and it will be opened to you. For everyone who asks receives, and he who seeks finds, and to him who knocks it will be opened" (Matthew 7:7–8).

Finally, open and close your study with prayer. Ask the Holy Spirit, whom Jesus called the Spirit of Truth, to guide your discussion and to reveal what is of eternal benefit to you individually and as a group. As you close your time together, ask the Holy Spirit to seal to your remembrance what you have read and studied, and to show you ways in the upcoming days, weeks, and months how to apply what you have studied to your daily life and relationships.

General Themes for the Lessons

Each lesson in this study has one or more core themes. Continually pull the group back to these themes. You can do this by asking simple questions, such as, "How does that relate to _____?" . . . "How does that help us better understand the concept of _____ ?" . . . "In what ways does that help us apply the principle of _____ ?"

A summary of general themes or concepts in each lesson follows:

Lesson #1
EFFECTIVE PRAYER FOR OTHERS
Praying for Unbelievers
Praying for Fellow Believers
Receiving the Prayers of Others

Lesson #2
THE SUPREMACY OF CHRIST JESUS
The Supremacy of Christ
The "Mystery" Aspect of Faith
Knowing ABOUT God vs. Knowing God
False God in Today's World
The Heresy of Multiple Paths to God

Lesson #3
THE LIMITATIONS OF LEGALISM
False Teachings Prevalent Today
Legalism
Religion vs. Relationship with Christ Jesus
Prerequisites for Salvation vs. Prudence of Witness

Lesson #4
PUTTING OFF THE OLD NATURE
Changing Behavioral and Attitudinal Pattern
Living "Heaven's Way" on Earth
Behaviors and Attitudes Unbecoming to a Christian

Lesson #5
PUTTING ON A NEW NATURE
Behaviors and Attitudes that Exalt Christ Jesus
Seeking Biblical Wisdom
Teaching Others
Admonishing Others, Especially in Song
The Importance of Giving Thanks

Lesson #6
THE CHRISTIAN HOME
Reciprocity of Obligation
The Challenges Facing Godly Wives
The Challenges Facing Godly Husband
The Challenges Facing Godly Parents
The Challenges Facing Godly Children
Doing All Things "As Unto the Lord"

Lesson #7

HOW TO TREAT THOSE WHO SERVE YOU OR RULE OVER YOU

Changing Systems vs. Transforming Lives

Being Profitable to Others

Seeing God's Plans and Purposes Even in Negative Situations

The Challenges Facing Godly Leaders and Employers

The Challenges Facing Godly Followers and Employees

The Importance of Justice and Fairness in Working Relationships

Being a Bondservant of Christ Jesus

NOTES

NOTES

NOTES

NOTES

NOTES

NOTES